AF373311

Marcus Deminco

Suffering is the best medicine to awaken
the spirit (Émile Zola)

Translated by Ilka Andrade Suarez
Copyright © 2020 - Marcus Deminco
All Rights Reserved | Salvador – Bahia – Brazil
ISBN: 9798653887697
Independently Published

Formatting, layout and conversion for eBooks
Marlon Bellator
md.bellator@gmail.com
Cover Creation
Erick Cerqueira (Marketing & Design)
http://esc3d.com.br

D395s

Deminco, Marcus

Ritalin VS. Attention Deficit Hyperactivity Disorder – Lies and Truths / Marcus Deminco – 1ª ed. – Salvador : Independently Published, 2020. Translated by Ilka Andrade Suarez
Marcus Deminco, 2020.
102 p.

ISBN: 9798653887697

1. Attention Deficit Hyperactivity Disorder. 2. Drug Treatment, Psychotropic, Psychostimulant. 3. Psychology. I. Title. Myths and Truths, ADHD – Attention Deficit Hyperactivity Disorder.
I.,. II. Título.

CDD-658.45
CDU: 811.134.3

Scheda di catalogazione preparata dal sistema bibliotecario universitario (SIBI / UFBA)

Ritalin
VS.
Attention Deficit Hyperactivity Disorder
−Lies and Truths−

Marcus Deminco

Marcus Deminco

Translated by Ilka Andrade Suarez
Copyright © 2020 - Marcus Deminco
All Rights Reserved | Salvador – Bahia – Brazil
ISBN: 9798653887697
Independently Published

Marcus Deminco

SUMMARY

Clarification Note

Currently, Attention Deficit Hyperactivity Disorder (**ADHD**) is estimated to affect 2.5% of adults, about 3 to 7% of school-age children (6-12 years) worldwide, and in More than 68% of cases the disorder lasts for life.

Considering these numbers, the high prevalence of **ADHD**, and with the objective of clarify the endless and controversial discussion about risks, the high increase in the consumption of the remedy in the country, and the probable effects of dependence on the use of the drug Ritalin (Methylphenidate) for the treatment of Hyperactivity Attention Deficit Disorder (**ADHD**), this book was prepared simply and interactively to provide that — after this brief reading — you can even expand your own opinion of risks, benefits, truths, and the lies concerning the use of the drug Ritalin as the substance of first choice for the treatment of **ADHD**.

The book also contains a list of some celebrities who own the Disorder and closes with exciting testimonials from people diagnosed with **ADHD**.

My Complaint

In the course of the first half of 2013, after more than four months without the distribution of Ritalin of 10 mg throughout the national territory, in the face of the accomplice silence of all those who should speak, I decided to express all my indignation. So, since you were going to expose me, as I tend to be exaggerated in the exact dismeasure, I certainly couldn't reveal anything just in half. In this way, and in accordance with Johann Goethe's wise words: "Man of common sense never commits a madness of little importance" — through an open email, made available on the Internet — on May 2 of that same year, I presented to the Federal Public Prosecutor's Office (MPF), a Complaint dealing with alleged irregularities practiced by the National Health Surveillance Agency (ANVISA), the Novartis Laboratory (Ritalin Manufacturer), and the indecorous action of some of the most renowned national experts in **ADHD.** I therefore reproduce below part of the pieces of information of my representation.

Dear (as) Mrs. (as). Good morning!

My name is Marcus Deminco. I am A Writer, Psychologist, Professor of Physical Education, Tutor of Neurolinguistic

Programming (NLP), Doctor Honoris Causa in **ADHD**, author of the book **Me And My Friend DDA - Autobiography Of A Carrier Of Attention Deficit Hyperactivity Disorder (ADHD)**, I have Attention Deficit Disorder with Hyperactivity, and also make use of Ritalin (Methylphenidate Hydrochloride). **Have any of you heard anything about it?** I'd rather assume not. For, only in this way, I can camouflage my certainty not to admit as probable, the coexistence of some negligent form of omission: nor in fancy of neglect and/or mischievous of ignorance. And while there are still some frets with a strong smell of collusion, I believe — only to appear the sympathy of a passive idiot — who heard about, possibly did not hear what they heard, or learned to hear from those who could not explain. And when you learn something wrong, with the certainty that you have known the right, inevitably you tend to commit countless misconceptions, however, without the slightest ability to discern what is wrong, since you do not know the right thing.

The worst, however, is when the presumption of thinking that one knows becomes greater than the awareness of seeing primitive mistakes. It tends to make new mistakes, in evolutionary and disproportionate proportions. And the moment something very serious happens -- as possibly happening now -- because they don't judge their neglected conduct instinctively, they'll go out looking for who was to blame for their mistakes. As Nietzsche said: *"Convictions are more dangerous enemies of truth than lies."*

Whenever I am invited by some vehicle of communication to grant an interview talking about **ADHD,** I end up facing some dangerous questions to be answered. Not just for its possible consequences, but mainly because they should be answered by some of you. However, if no one has said anything so far about what they have always talked so much, I dare to speak for your muteness. Yes, as Luther King said: "Cowardice raises the question: **Is it Safe?** Entrepreneurship raises the question: **Is it Popular?** The label raises the question: **Is it Elegant?** But consciousness raises the question: **Is it Right?** And it comes to a time when we have to take a position that is not safe, it is not elegant, it is not popular, but we have to do it because our conscience tells us that this is the Right **Attitude".**

So, following the cries of my moral conscience, in respect of disrespect that — both the National Health Surveillance Agency (ANVISA) and Novartis and its "sponsored patrons" — are disregarding the millions of Brazilians who have hyperactivity care deficit disorder**,** along with their families, I decided to meet the uncontrollable appeals of my frontal orbit cortex and write them openly. So — in addition to trying to elucidate some questions that should have already been clarified — you could take the opportunity to define a sober answer, among no sensible people who can report how what never happened. Or maybe -- as who knows what you don't know -- may still be able to explain the inexplicable.

Admitting, beforehand, my totally ignorant juridicity. But,

ignorantly aware of the seriousness of the facts, I respectfully request the **Federal Public Prosecutor's Office (MPF)** to determine how much really exists, among all of these my presupposition presented in the text below. Above all, regarding the facts inserted in the links of topics **2** and **3**:

1. About the lack of Ritalin 10 mg and the contradictory justifications.

While in a statement Novartis stated that the lack of the drug occurred due to a "delay" in the import permits of the **active ingredient**, a Biologist at Novartis phoned me saying that the problem was due to the "delay" in the authorization of the says, and by email, an official claimed that the "delay" would have been due to an ANVISA. The 'delay' always used by them as a euphemism of lack - both of medicine and respect - was still blamed for a fire of extremely devastating proportions. And despite this fact resembling the disrepute of the preceding miscreants, it was perhaps the only truth in this great trolley.

Although I was slightly perplexed to find a lost truth beneath so many liars, what made me even more impressed was the personality of fire. His flame was really determined to counter logic: he selected, separated, picked and chose to burn, only solid tablets with 10 mg Ritalin filling particles, to the setback of capsules coated by sucrose balls, copolymer of ammonium methacrylate, methacrylic acid copolymer, etc. of the LA Ritalins. Was the fire independent of reason or so dependent on drugs like that?

1.1 After concrete lies came abstract truths.

On April 16, 2013 — in another response pasted and for the many other complaints available on the site: *Complain Here,* someone from Novartis stated that regularization was scheduled for the last week of April. Just four days later, they made a statement available through the internet, presenting a new justification that also did not justify anything new, making it obvious that the delay had not been due to all the other previous lies. The new statement contradicted what they had said: the national market refueling forecast changed from last week to the end of May 2013.

In reciprocity the such lack of respect, on June 26, through this same site, I demonstrated that we often speak playing just as a gentle way of telling some truths without being offensive. However, I knew that this technique should never be practiced towards those who are not even kidding able to reveal some truth. And as a neglect does not match any expression of joke, without the slightest concern to be kind, and already aware that i would have no access to that information so rusty, I thought that by debauchery —at least — they would ridicule them as part of the my indignation. And instead of the complaint I preferred the trocist inquiry:

Dear (a) Mr. (a) So-and-so (a) of Tal.

If daily, for 9 years Joãozinho used 4 tablets of the drug Ritalin of

10 mg, but suddenly, enjoying the sovereign autonomy that the non-observance of ANVISA granted them, the Novartis Laboratory decided to simply interrupt its supply for almost 5 months. Fearful of possible adverse reactions (inserted in the medicine's own package leaflet) Joãozinho decides to buy Ritalin without a prescription on the black market. Below is the alternative corresponding to who would have committed the most serious crime:

a) The Novartis Laboratory

b) The ANVISA

c) Johnny

d) Who sold the drug that hadn't even gotten into the story?

e) NAA (None of the Answers Above)

Also, that same day, without pointing out any of the alternatives proposed by me, I obtained as a response from the company:

Dear (a) sir(a),
We appreciate the contact and inform you that this message box is used exclusively to assist the internal areas of ANVISA and the entities of the national health surveillance system, as well as for the receipt of some emails with attachment.
For greater speed and control:
In case of complaints, complaints, suggestions or compliments, please fill out the electronic form by accessing the link: http://www1.anvisa.gov.br/ouvidoria/cadastroprocedimentointernetact.do?metodo=inicia

• In case of information, questions or requests for views and copies of processes/documents, please contact the telephone call center 0800-6429782;

• In case of scheduling meetings of companies with technical areas, please access the parlatory system;

- Matches:

Anvisa
SIA Excerpt 05 Special Area 57
ZIP Code: 71.205-050
Brasilia - DF
Best regards
Ombudsman/ANVISA
This is an automatic message. Please not answer.

I often don't know how far some people are going to understand **ADHD**, however, after reading something so alienating like that, I'm also not able to predict how far other ignorance can get. It was clear that I would not respond again, which would be expendable to ask me for the favor of what already seemed logical to me: not to respond to an automatic message. But as it is carefully used in a message to express that the sender devotes all attention to the subject, I also did not understand how an automatic email could have been considerate.

Later, without any plausible justification, the laboratory began to demonstrate wanting to know only from that fact, everything they should know long before. And delayed with logic, some complaints began to respond emphasizing a concern as excessive as alienated: they even forgotten the very adverse effects in the bull.

(a) As in your message reference to "... have interrupted is hurting me a lot...", in order to provide safety to consumers, we would like to receive more information about it, so if possible, we ask you to contact us on 0800 888 3003, option 2 , (Monday to Friday from 8 am to p.m.) and enter the case number 01006206.1.

(b) As in his message makes the reference "My son became aggressive in the first few weeks and now faces a DRASTIC REDUCTION IN SCHOOL INCOME" during treatment with Novartis drug, in order to provide safety to consumers we would like to receive more information regarding, so if possible, please contact us on 0800 888 3003, option 2, (Monday to Friday, 08:00 to 17:00) and please inform us the case number 01003269.

(c) As in your message makes the reference "... I feel frustrated with relying on a medicine..." during treatment with Novartis medicinal product, in order to provide safety to consumers we would like to receive more information about, so if possible, we ask you to contact us on 0800 888 3003, option 2 , (Monday to Friday, from 08:00 to 17h) and enter the case number 01000457.

Thus, I was absorbed among the most varied doubts: Were they attendants in the initial period of training who answered the emails, were we talking about the same medication, or had they never read the package leaflet before? And as for the lack of 10 mg Ritalin:

a) Would it be due to the absence of Methylphenidate (active principle)?

b) For the lack of Salt (Hydrochloride)?

c) For lack of respect?

d) Does Novartis biologist understand biology less than I do?

e) Has ANVISA finally decided to realize the prognosis already known and warned by any less renowned and more expert specialist, less committed to its partisanship and more committed to people?

f) Or are all previous alternatives correct?

2. ANVISA vs. NOVARTIS — Was there crime?

In the country where we are much more charged for the fulfilments of duties, we end up little knowing about our rights. Aside from that not all rights, among the few we know, will actually serve something. I therefore appeal here to the Public Prosecutor's Office to evaluate, relight and/or rectify all my possible misconceptions.

The following Art. 10 of Provisional Measure No. 2,190-34 of 23 August 2001 in its item XXXIX is still in force?

> Discontinue, suspend or reduce, without just cause, the production or distribution of red stripe medicines, continuous use or essential to the health of the individual, or black stripe, causing the market to be defueled: penalty - warning, total or partial prohibition of the establishment, cancellation of the registration of the product, cancellation of authorization for the operation of the company, cancellation of the licensing license of the establishment and / or fine.

Assuming that a dumb bird in a lucid auditory hallucination has confided in good Portuguese that the last batch of the drug

Ritalin 10 mg was already dating its manufacture on Nov/2012. However, without having to prove, because the bird besides mute has Social Phobia and does not talk to strangers. But if any competent body finds that the silent bird was telling the truth would it be clear that the lab already knew that the drug would be missing? And already knowing that it would be lacking, his anarchism also exempts him from the fulfillment of Art. 10 of Provisional Measure No. 2,190-34 in issue XL?

> Fail to communicate to the health surveillance body of the Ministry of Health the interruption, suspension or reduction of the manufacture or distribution of the medicines referred to in item XXXIX: penalty - warning, total or partial prohibition of the establishment, cancellation of the registration of the product, cancellation of authorization for the operation of the company, cancellation of the licensing permit of the establishment and / or fine;

And if we confront the two respective statements, inserted in the bull of Ritalin **(a)** and **(b)** with the unique paragraph of Art. 20. Cap. VI of LAW No. 9,782 of January 26, 1999, or would the Paragraph included by Decree No. 3,961 of 10.10.2001 be the most correct?

(a) Its mechanism of action in man has not yet been fully elucidated;

(b) Safety and efficacy data on the use of Long-Term Ritalin are not complete;

Unique paragraph of Art. 20. Cap. VI of LAW No. 9,782 of January 26, 1999:

> The drug which does not have in its composition is known to be beneficial from a clinical or therapeutic point of view may be recorded.
>
> § 1ᵗʰᵉ only drug containing in its composition a substance admittedly beneficial from a clinical and therapeutic point of view may be recorded. (Paragraph included by Decree No. 3,961 of 10 October 2001).

Aware that in Brazil there is no remuneration for guinea pigs, would we be paying to be guinea pigs without knowing? Also stressing that it was not the first time Novartis acted irresponsibly, uncompromisingly and fully independently. In 2011, on the pretext of the change in packaging to provide higher product quality resolved — with the sovereign autonomy that the non-compliance granted them — cease the supply of the medically between May and June, when they returned supply only with aluminum *blisters* and the format of the modified box. They would have acted in confluence to Art's Inciso XVI. 3rd decree No. 3,961, From October 10, 2001 (Amends Decree No. 79,094, Of January 5, 1977, Regulating Law No. 6,360, September 23, 1976):

> Label — Printed, lithographed, painted, stored, fire-engraved, pressure or self-adhesive identification applied directly to containers, packaging, wrappers or any external or internal packaging protector and cannot be removed or altered during use of the product and during its transport or storage.

And as for the warnings described in the bull: Do not interrupt treatment without the knowledge of your doctor. Withdrawal of the drug can lead to depression and consequences of hyperactivity. Would they be doctors of all **ADHD** carriers in Brazil without knowing, were the culprits ourselves for not warning them that we would stop treatment, or would Novartis have once again violated the law? According to Art. 148 of Decree No. 3,961 of 10 October 2001:

> § 1 (o) Registration undertakings, manufacturers or importers have a responsibility to ensure and ensure that the quality, safety and efficacy of products are maintained to the final consumer in order to avoid risks and adverse health effects.

I ALSO SUGGEST that someone more competent and/or with greater legal knowledge analyze other aspects that can be considered as criminals under in accordance with Decree No. 3,961, October 10, 2001.

2.1. What about the other losses?

In the hands of who dot patients and/or their families should take the blank check that can pay off the unknown value of this debt? Who will pay the bills arising from this injury, if the amounts are as incalculable as the calculations you submit intermittently, you present? Which of the institutions can repair the moral damage caused by neglect with the lives of these people?

I, for example, hit my car twice in a single week. And in addition to the explanations that won't solve the problems, I'm waiting for the standalone remedy, a fine for overcoming —without realizing what I realized—the sign closed. Although I don't even remember if I really crossed some signal. Something even common in the lives of many people with **ADHD.** As stated by the International *Consensus Statement on ADHD* (2002):

> Experts warn that people with **ADHD** have difficulty adhering to social laws and rules and are more subject to accidents and undesirable situations such as early pregnancy, sexually transmitted diseases, traffic fines, marital conflicts and depression.

Disregarding my fine and considering **ADHD** carriers with predominance of inattention that are run over on streets close to reality, but away from statistics. Adding to the predominantly hyperactive-impulsive type victims in car accidents due to speeding in immeasurable indices. How will they know how many of them may lose, or have already lost their lives for the irresponsibility of two institutions without defined hierarchies, nor ethical precepts established in their practical actions?

Studies by Barkley (2002) have shown that throughout development, the life of a child with **ADHD** is permeated by many failures. In general, these children have great risks of expulsions and school suspensions, higher chances of repetition, school dropout, difficult relationships, conduct problems, development of anxiety, depression, low self-esteem, drug involvement and learning problems. When there is a comorbidity picture, this picture may have even more lifelong implications. So how will they reimburse those who have lost a discipline at school, those who have been disapproved in an important test, eliminated in a job selection? And who will pay for the new private consultations that will have to be rescheduled due to expired revenues?

3. Didn't ANVISA know?

3.1. Let us look at the prognosis first by the psychopathological aspects of **ADHD** itself. The Diagnostic and Statistical Manual of Mental Disorders (DSM-IV) in its 4th edition rcinforces:

> Impulsivity can lead to accidents (e.g. tearing down objects, colliding with people, inadvertently holding a hot pot) and engaging in potentially dangerous activities, without regard to possible consequences (e.g. skateboarding on extremely uneven terrain). Individuals with this disorder are easily distracted by irrelevant stimuli and usually interrupt ongoing tasks to pay attention to noises or trivial events that are generally easily ignored by others (e.g., the horn of a car, a conversation in the background). I also add the weightless curiosity, the desire to want everything, the intolerance the routine and the search for new adventures.

3.2. As for the comorbidities present in ADHD, Tannock (2000) warns:

> People with **ADHD** have a higher tendency to abuse drugs. The index can reach 50%. In the case of treatment of chemical dependents, it is essential to investigate whether **ADHD** is diagnosed. One can use alcohol, marijuana and tranquilizers as a way to anesthetize their negative thoughts, depression, agitation and chronic anxiety. It's behavior that leads to immediate gratification. In the short term they may even function as relief because unpredictable gratification releases more dopamine, but chronic use leads to depression, total demotivation, and disorganization takes care of the

person. It can use amphetamine, caffeine and cocaine as a concentration instrument of mental clarity.

3.3. We now correlated the above information with the chemical formulas of Ritalin and Cocaine:

a) F. Q — Ritalin (Methylphenidate): $\mathbf{C_{14}H_{19}NO_2}$.

b) F. Q — Cocaine: $\mathbf{C_{17}H_{21}NO_4}$.

I highlight, however, that although the two substances are Dopamine Reuptake Inhibitors (DRI), Methylphenidate acts more in modulating dopamine levels than Norepinephrine.

3.4. Also, in October 2004, in its issue of No. 1877 veja magazine highlighted: "One of the most worrying aspects of the use of Ritalin is recreational. Some teenagers grind the drágeas and smell the dust. Others dilute the tablet in water to inject it into the vein [...]".

3.5. They became aware in June 2011:

> The National Health Surveillance Agency is studying, in the coming months, to make it illegal to sell appetite-inhibiting drugs containing sibutramine or amphetamine derivatives such as Fenproporex, Mazindol and Amfepramone. The measure is commendable, since it draws attention to the important fight against the medicalization of society, a flag assumed by CRP-RJ since 2006, but at the same time worrying, because it does not include the fight against the indiscriminate use of Ritalin.(ANVISA studies banning amphetamines, but Ritalin sits out. Article was published in the 32nd edition of the Journal of CRP - http://tinyurl.com/6djsndr).

3.6. On its page on Methylphenidate <u>Wikipedia</u> describes between the ways of administration of the drug, oral, transdermal and **nasal**.

3.7. With the title *Abuse of Ritalín en young men* a video posted on <u>Youtube</u>, dated September 15, 2010 - a young man demonstrates how easy it is to crush Ritalin's tablet with a spoon to later inhale.

3.8. Aside from so many other information available to those who see what they look at. In Ritalin's own bull, for example, at least three subliminal information makes it even more implicit:

a) Among the adverse reactions: Inflammation of the nasal pathways and throat;

b) Nasopharyngitis (without explaining the meaning in the bull). It is an acute or chronic inflammation of the nasal mucosa;

c) In the passage referring to the procedure in cases of overdose, when they mention that "if the overdose is oral", they indicate that there are other routes of administration.

3.9. It is worth noting that, although I have a certain affinity with everything to what is strange, realizing that some things were much stranger than my affinity, since February 2011, I had already sent an email to ANVISA (Protocol No. 2011047296) questioning another obscured aspect:

Dear (a) Mr. (a) ANVISA attendant,

I have Attention Deficit Hyperactivity Disorder **(ADHD)** and for six years I have been using the only two national psychoactive drugs based on Methylphenidate: RITALIN (Novartis) and CONCERTA (Janssen-Cilag). However, aside from some less widespread psychotropic drugs for **ADHD** and that are not sold in Brazil (Focalin, Daytrana, Adderall, Vyvanse, Dexedrine etc.), Would you like to know why STRATTERA (Atomoxetine),manufactured by Eli Lilly, available in the USA for eight years and scheduled to launch for Brazil since 2004, until today is not marketed in our pharmacies?

After all, given the numerous measures taken by ANVISA in order to reduce the indiscriminate consumption of medicines - especially of drugs - it is at least contradictory that, being the only drug approved for the treatment of ADHD that does not belong to the class of psychostimulants, sold without Special Prescription (type A checkbook), with studies proving lower risks of dependence, and can be administered with a single dose daily, STRATTERA (Atomoxetine) is banned in Brazil.

Best regards without attention,

Marcus Deminco

3.10. Getting as an answer something that didn't match reality much. At least, at least I know *atomoxetine* does not belong to the class of psychostimulants and is therefore sold worldwide with simple prescription.

Dear (a) Lord(a),

In mind your request, we inform you that the drug Strattera is in the process of registering by this Agency. However, we inform you that if this medicine is registered, it will be prescribed only by a prescription in a special talonary, type A.

Best regards

Anvisa Meets

Call Center

National Health Surveillance Agency

0800 642 9782

www.anvisa.gov.br

3.11. Even without understanding all the lack of understanding of what might not even be understood, something even more incomprehensible was able to untangle me after so many embarrassments:

> Strattera (Atomoxetine) cannot be marketed in Brazil. However, ANVISA allows it to be used on national soil. As long as you bought out of the country. Considering that ANVISA presents as its mission: protection and promotion to the health of the population. It is assumed by obviousness — obviously dubious that — would never allow the use of Atomoxetine if the drug offered any health risk. Therefore, why indeed, or why no reason is in fact conditioned to its deprivation in Brazil (only in pharmacies) since 2004?

So, **Strattera** (Atomoxetine) that is not marketed in Brazil can be imported, but can 10 mg Ritalin - sovereign on the national market since 1988 — not even in case of absence be imported? Should I understand anything? It would be important to clarify all this right, perhaps someone would want to know if there is any special recipe to be able to import Heroin directly from the Red-Light *District* in Amsterdam.

3.12. Just wanting to understand something intelligible about what I would be one of the most interested, I still found some almost as explicable coincidences to be just coincidences. Casually, the only two first-choice drugs for **ADHD** in Brazil (with the same active ingredient Methylphenidate) belonged to the two Pharmaceutical Industries among the most powerful in the world. Both Ritalin from **Novartis** biosciences laboratory and Concerta, from the **Janssen-Cilag laboratory, which is a** subsidiary of Johnson & Johnson. In 2007, on the list of the 10 largest pharmaceutical industries in revenue volume, Novartis ranked 2nd while Johnson **& Johnson** was in 6th place. (*Top 50 Pharmaceutical Companies & Lists, Med Ad News, September 2007*). Among the 15 pharmaceutical companies that sold the most in 2008, the **Novartis** laboratory was 3rd place and Johnson **& Johnson** was 7th. (IMS Health 2008, Top 15 Global Corporations). In the report released by financial times global *500* (2011) with the ranking of the 225 largest companies in the world (not just pharmaceutical companies), Johnson **& Johnson** appeared in 25th place, **Novartis** in 32nd and far from them, in 184th place appeared the Eli Lilly and **Company**. Perhaps these data explain why **Strattera** (Atomoxetine) until today cannot be marketed in national pharmacies.

3.13. Forgetting that in Brazil, cancer medicine has already been falsified and contraceptive stemmed from wheat flour pills, is it even that Atomoxetine, used in the USA for more than 10 years, would not go through ANVISA's strict quality system or are there bureaucratic obstacles in front of our health? By the way, what's missing for us to produce or import some Ritalin Generics 10 mg? There are several Methylphenidates of 10 mg in several countries:

Attenta, Medikinet, Metadate, Methylin, Penid, Rubifen, Focalin. (correct me if some of these are already marketed here in Brazil).

I also don't know if they already know, but there are generics of long-lasting Methylphenidate: Watson Methylphenidate ER (generic USA), Teva-Methylphenidate ER-C (generic Canadian), Equasym XL, Medikinet XL, Metadate CD, Rubifen SR.

And according to Law No. 8,080 of September 19, 1990, in its Art. 6, § 1:

> Health surveillance means a set of actions capable of eliminating, reducing or preventing health risks and intervening in health problems arising from the environment, the production and circulation of goods and the provision of services of interest to health, Covering:
>
> I. The control of consumer goods that, directly or indirectly, relate to health, understood all stages and processes, from production to consumption;
>
> II. The control of the provision of services that relates directly or indirectly to health.

According to Art. 1º The National Health Surveillance System comprises the set of actions defined by § 1 of Art. 6 and Art. 15 to 18 of Law No. 8,080 of September 19, 1990, executed by institutions of direct and indirect Public Administration of the Union, States, the Federal District and municipalities, which carry out regulatory, standardization, control and supervision activities in the health surveillance area.

Art, art. 2º It is up to the Union under the National Health Surveillance System:

I. Define the national health surveillance policy;

II. Define the National Health Surveillance System;

III. Standardize, control and supervise products, substances and services of interest to health;

IV. Exercise the sanitary surveillance of ports, airports and borders, and this assignment may be exercised by the States, the Federal District and the Municipalities;

V. Monitor and coordinate state, district and municipal health surveillance actions;

VI. Provide technical and financial cooperation to states, the Federal District and municipalities;

VII. Act in special circumstances of health risk;

VIII. Maintain information system in health surveillance, in cooperation with states, the Federal District and municipalities.

In addition to the legal precepts, would the National Health Surveillance Agency (ANVISA) have fulfilled its Mission?

> Promote and protect the health of the population and intervene in the risks arising from the production and use of products and services subject to health surveillance, in coordinated action with the states, municipalities and the Federal District, according to the principles of the Single System of health, to improve the quality of life of the Brazilian population.

And, what about their vision?

To be legitimized by society as an institution integral to the Unified Health System, agile, modern and transparent, of national and international reference in regulation and sanitary control.

Would they have followed the precepts of their values?

- Ethics and responsibility as a public agent.
- Ability to articulate and integrate.
- Excellence in management.
- Knowledge as a source for action.
- Transparency.
- Accountability.

4. Regarding the excess in methylphenidate consumption in Brazil.

Why did methylphenidate consumption rise 75% from 2009 to 2011? If from Set. /2007 to Oct./2008 were sold 1,238,064 boxes, while from Set. /2011 to Oct./ 2012 sales increased to 1,853,930 boxes, there are some reasons — at least — reasonably obvious to this.

Although some renowned experts need to say anyway, through any miraculously invented mathematics, that there was no excess. He stated, even that due to the prevalence of **ADHD,** even with these 1,853,930 boxes, more than three million carriers would be untreated in the country. I believe that perhaps, even by the need to invent justifiable statistics, they end up ignoring other data: if for each psychotropic box sold in Brazil, two are acquired illegally, and if I'm not mistaken (although sometimes they even fool me), the

Methylphenidates provided to the SUS are also not accounted for as they can assert these numbers if they don't even exist?

First, to see if there is an excess in methylphenidate consumption in Brazil, it would be necessary to know the number of people diagnosed and how many of them are being treated with Methylphenidate. Subsequently, verifying that the increase in consumption would have been higher than the prevalence of **ADHD.** The problem, however, begins exactly from there: data on the prevalence of **ADHD** in Brazil, mostly, are manipulated and disseminated in booklets and/or pseudo *articles* sponsored by the pharmaceutical industries themselves. Would you contradict your boss? Well, neither do they.

For Miguelote (2008) as economic production began to depend on science as value, the articulation between the pharmaceutical industry and the knowledge industry was configured in a powerful gear sustained by marketing strategies. Thus, the production of medical knowledge, scientifically legitimate through research, feeds the production of articles, while ensuring circulation of knowledge and sale of medicines. According to the same author, most clinical trials to test new drugs or new procedures, sponsored by industry, are made from protocols that are prepared and analyzed by the sponsor. The researcher receives the function of recruiting patients. The physicians interviewed stated that they received remuneration per patient captured without access to data analysis or preparation of the article. In some surveys, the value is preestablished and monthly.

> We note that potential conflicts of interest to publications are rarely mentioned. Only eight scientific articles make the funding of the manufacturer's laboratories explicit. Another item just appreciates the funding of the manufacturer laboratory. Researching, in each article, each author observed that the number of articles that should present conflicts of interest because they receive funding from laboratories, or because they co-authored the manufacturers, would be 27 articles, representing 87% of the scientific articles analyzed [...] We believe that the veiled financing of manufacturers laboratories in almost all publications on the uses of Methylphenidate is a serious ethical issue and requires greater care in accepting results. Why are these funding repeatedly denied? Articles that are not sponsored by laboratories correspond practically to articles that do not address the theme of **ADHD.** The research groups on **ADHD** in Brazil are all sponsored by the manufacturers of the products. But how does this relationship between economic interests and health actions look like? The dissemination of Brazilian scientific research on the uses of Methylphenidate seems to be subordinate to commercial interests that constantly insist on denying. (ORTEGA, F. et al., 2010).

In addition to some 'enlightening campaigns' carried out within schools. As Tainah Medeiros pointed out, through an article available on Dr. Drauzio Varella's website published on 03/10/2013:

> Contrary to minimizing the concern that should be spent on the diagnosis of the disorder, there are rumors that Novartis pharmacist will campaign in schools warning about the risks of **ADHD** and guiding on ways to identify it. For many, this would justify the greater amount of diagnoses and,

consequently, the greater use of Ritalin in recent years. During an interview with Drauzio Varella, the existence of such campaigns was vehemently denied by the pharmacist. In 2010, however, Novartis and ABDA (Brazilian Association of Attention Deficit) promoted the "Professor Attention" competition, which aimed to "help educators know and better deal with **ADHD**". To take the prize of R $ 7 thousand it was necessary to present the best proposals for inclusion of **ADHD** carriers in the classroom. In addition to the value, schools would earn a kit containing a champagne, an Inclusion Project School Certificate and a trophy. The project leader would receive nominal support to participate in a National Congress in the area of education, "contemplating passage, lodging and registration in the maximum amount of R$ 4,000.00". Three schools were drawn. Novartis denied any involvement with educational projects inside and outside schools, although the project seeks to assist in the recognition and conduct of the disorder and that the official page of the contest display the company's signature as one of the responsible for the initiative.

IN FACT, does this type of marketing have a legitimate character, or violate Art. 199 of the Federal Constitution?

Health care is free to private initiative.

§ 3 - The direct or indirect participation of foreign companies or capitals in health care in the country is prohibited, except in the cases provided for by law. In addition to failing to comply with Provisional Measure No. 2,190-34 / 2001— in its regard V: advertise products under sanitary surveillance, food and others, contrary to health legislation.

It is also considered, as another serious ethical issue, the close link between renowned experts and the Novartis Pharmaceutical Laboratory. Not by chance, they are the same producers of *funded pseudo articles,* responsible for defining what **ADHD** is on the Laboratory's Own Website.

Thus, **ANVISA** would be acting in confluence to Decree No. 3,571 of August 21, 2000. Art, art. 3° XXVI in what it values: *control, supervise and monitor, from the perspective of health legislation, the advertising and advertising of products submitted to the health surveillance regime?*

4.1 CONCLUSION:

It is impossible to know if there really is an excess in methylphenidate consumption in Brazil, without knowing the amount of the drug being used for the treatment of cases of Narcolepsy and Idiopathic Hypersomnia, the number of people diagnosed who are being treated with Methylphenidate, "guessing" (since it cannot be known) how many boxes are acquired illegally, have access to the amount of Methylphenidate provided to the SUS that are not accounted for, to only then, correlate all this data with the prevalence of **ADHD** in the country.

5. Suggestions for **NOVARTIS**.

5.1. NEVER confuse Attention Deficit Hyperactivity Disorder (ADHD) as some synonym for idiotic, retarded or demented;

5.2. NEVER ask a person with **ADHD** to call a number 0800 that no one answers;

5.3. When you don't have something sober, true, or objective to answer **NEVER** copy and collect the same answer to all questions sent by email.

5.4. Try to learn more about the medicines they sell;

5.5. Also insert into the Ritalin bull: **Stopping the Drug can cause damage to Novartis itself;**

6. Suggestions for ANVISA.

6.1. Hyperactivity Attention Deficit Disorder **(ADHD)** is something very serious to be treated with neglect size and disrespect;

6.2. Undoubtedly — after all — Methylphenidate is even the best psychotropic (not the only one) for **ADHD** Treatment. However, we cannot be at the mercy since 1988 only from a Pharmaceutical Industry as devoid as Novartis.

6.3. After all, in addition to STRATTERA (Atomoxetine), the first drug not belonging to the psychostimulant class, officially approved in the USA for the treatment of **ADHD** in children, adolescents and adults, with a planned launch in Brazil since 2004, what is also missing to import the Generics of Ritalin of 10mg, such as Attenta, Medikinet, Metadate, Methylin, Penid, Rubifen, Focalin? What about the generics of long-term Methylphenidate, such as Watson Methylphenidate ER, Teva-Methylphenidate ER-C, Equasym XL, Medikinet XL, Metadate CD, Rubifen SR?

6.4. However, if they wish to reduce and/or curb non-drug use (especially recreational use) if the tablets cannot be coated, check for other EXCIPIENTS chemically compatible with Methylphenidate. **For example,** if 10 mg Ritalin EXCIPIENTs are: tricacic phosphate, lactose, starch, gelatin, magnesium stearate and talc. Perhaps it does not modify so much exchange them for magnesium stearate, starch, sodium croscarmelosis, lactose or sodium croscarmelosis, hypromelose, povidona, glycerol stearate palmitate, microcrystalline cellulose, macrogol, titanium dioxide and macrogol 400.

7. Message to the "REPUTED" experts.

Even without citing their renames, certainly many will know how to recognize them among the sudden silence of good convenience. However, defending, supporting, fighting and **PROFITING** for a cause with such laxity is like being a soldier without uniform in the middle of a battlefield waiting for the army with greater artillery power to migrate, even if the other has far more soldiers. Perhaps it's even the best war strategy, but it will certainly never be the most honorable.

For the most interested I would also recommend reading the following articles:

1) Ritalin in Brazil: productions, discourses and practices. Available from:
http://www.scielo.br/pdf/icse/v14n34/aop1510.pdf

2) Ritalin in Brazil: A decade of production, dissemination and consumption. Available from:
http://www.ebookcult.com.br/produto/A_Ritalina_no_Brasil_uma_decada_de_producao_divulgacao_e_consumo-50964

3) Marked Recipe and the admirable world of Ritalin. Available from:
http://oarquivo.lamia.kinghost.net/index.php?option=com_content&view=article&id=340

5:receita-marcada-e-o-admiravel-mundo-da-Ritalina-parte-1&catid=84:verdades-incovenientes-&Itemid=66

The Contradictory News About ADHD and Ritalin

Suddenly, several celebrities from all over the world diagnosed with Hyperactivity Attention Deficit Disorder (**ADHD**) have begun to make public details about their lives and experiences with the Disorder. Among the famous, Steve Jobs, Bill Gates, Steven Spielberg, Tom Cruise, Jim Carrey, Justin Timberlake, Will Smith, Danny Glover, Sylvester Stallone, Michael Jordan, Michael Phelps, Simone Biles, etc.

Consequently, **ADHD** began to symbolize a much less derogatory condition than those primitive ideas linked to limitations and/or disabilities. While possessing the Disorder, it even acquired a certain "status" of intelligence, of prodigiousness. As being a more frequent condition among differentiated, talented, creative people, extraordinary athletes, etc.

However, if the then watch that had never measured my time in accordance with the ordinary chronology of other men was finally synchronized; if just at that moment, perhaps for the first time in my entire life, I was in the perfect agreement with the events of the contemporary world, I had little time to enjoy that unpretentious punctuality of mine. For almost simultaneously, there were also beginning to emerge numerous matters trying to unframe me, leaving me out of the only situation in which I had not delayed myself. As if they wanted to put me back in the post of retarder, several factoids began to disclose that that disorder I had, already diagnosed eleven years ago, but now in full fashion, on the most favorable occasion, would simply not exist.

However, among the most varied fabulated news, some deserve — even in mutual lack of worthiness — a certain highlight. During the first half of 2013, for example, a headline replicated by several media outlets questioned and answered at the same time: "Why did French children lack attention deficit? " In their descriptive content, the reports claimed — with the property of those who could at most assume that — educational philosophy, along with a holistic psychosocial approach by French mental health experts — made hyperactivity Care Deficit Disorder **(ADHD)** simply disappear, or be able to reduce its incidence in tiny numbers.

But how to ignore one's own ignorance is the main feature of the ignorant, driven by an irrational urge to slight bare all his stupidity, these journalists, columnists, bloggers and so many other functional illiterate, self-educated by the presumption of what they think they know -- without even knowing for sure what they think -- they didn't even bother to investigate the origin of these sources, or to find out —even if it was through a quick google search — the veracity of the blunders before they reproduce. But, as Aristotle says, "The ignorant says, the wise man doubts, and the sensible reflects." And while I don't sympathize too much with wisdom, sometimes — even by tantrum — I'm stubborn enough, to the point of acting in complete disagreement with what I myself dislike, just to eventually be able to reflect weightlessly:

After all, why would there be a French Attention Deficit Association if the disorder wasn't even frequent there? Or why would a Facebook page (Hyper Supers — **ADHD** France) with more than 18,000 members, founded since February 5, 2002 with the Mission to Help People Affected by Hyperactivity Attention Deficit Disorder **(ADHD)?** Would the experts of the French Association of Attention Deficit in the absence of people with ADHD, be attending, producing scientific articles, providing informative services, and guiding hyperactive insects?

Other reports -- no less irresponsible and equally fanciful -- claimed that several young people would be using Ritalin (Methylphenidate Hydrochloride) in order to become more lit, and well-disposed to parties such as *Raves* and Carnivals. In one of these subjects, they even mentioned the case of a young nurse who claimed to feel yummy, beautiful, and with a sense of power — as well as experiencing a shiver as if preceding an orgasm — every time he took the drug. Another subject claimed to make use of the medicine before going out to ballads, ensuring that under the influence of Ritalin he already arrived at parties kissing everyone.

I confess —with the contradictory sarcasm of the seriousness of those who would confess something really important —that in the face of all these cases, I was ironically worried: or they would be selling me the counterfeit medicine, or that pill I was taking daily, for so many years, it would be any other remedy except that Ritalin with so many magical powers. First, because by pharmacodynamics itself, its substance causes much more a pathetic effect than excitatory. At least, it is how it works in my body the active ingredient of Ritalin that I make use of. According to that, indolent, with decreased sexual desire, xerostomia (dryness of the mouth), worsening of sociability, greater tendency to irritability, in addition to the effect known as "tunnel vision" (when the person holds so intensely in something, that ignores all other things and people around them), do not seem to be sensations of the nicest, nor so libidinous so for someone to want to go around buzzing with enthusiastic size.

As if enough were not much, or as if the much was not yet enough, time in another was reproduced, on numerous web pages that had nothing more useful to disclose, that same old news, outdated and already disproved for years: the image of a burlesque gentleman, illustrating the title: "Dr. Leon Eisenberg, the father of **ADHD**, said just before his death that **ADHD** is a fictitious disease".

Leaving aside, all incoherence inserted in the sayings that they make up of this news. After all, a father declaring that his own son would be a fiction invented by himself, it was at least something quite misplaced to already credit, in advance, so much truthfulness about the content of the news. However, whenever time was left to the setback of missing, I ended up not containing myself in replicating some of these sites. In one of these —through the space intended for criticism, suggestions and comments — I decided to give back to your columnist, a pharmaceutical and biochemistry consultant.

Initially, I stated that in translating the original text into German, she (or some other equally incompetent translator) had modified all the veracity of the facts: in what was actually said, at the place where it was said, when it was said, and by whom it was said. For example, the title itself does not match the truth, nor with the information reported by herself in the discussion of her own text: "Confession of deathbed of the inventor of **ADHD** : **ADHD** is a fictitious disease [...] At the age of 87 and seven months before his death, **ADHD's** scientific father stated in his last interview: **ADHD** is an excellent example of fictitious disease."

First, because the claim that Dr. Leon Eisenberg would have declared this would put the date of his utterance around February 2009. However, as for the documentation for putative quotation is provided in English, the statement that **ADHD** would be a manufactured disease, refers to an interview conducted on August 2, 2012 with Harvard University Professor of Psychology, Dr. Jerome Kagan. And with the title, Spiegel Interview with Jerome Kagan: What about Tutoring Instead of Pills? (What about Explanations instead of pills?), was it enough only a single answer

(1.2) of the interviewee to, at last and finally, disprove that news so plagiarized, lagging, recurrent and that filled the bag of any and all **ADHD** carriers.

1.1 Spiegel: Experts say that 5.4 million American children have typical **ADHD** symptoms. Are you saying that this mental disorder is just an invention?

1.2 Kagan: That's correct; it's an invention. Every child who is not doing well at school is sent to see a pediatrician, and the pediatrician says, "It's **ADHD,** here's Ritalin. "In fact, 90% of these 5.4 million children do not have an abnormal dopamine metabolism. The problem is that if the drug is available to doctors, they will make the corresponding diagnosis.

While another article -- not aired through the site but reproduced by *the Newspaper Der Spiegel* -- made it clear that Dr. Eisenberg at no point stated that   **ADHD** was an unreal disorder. In fact, he had said only that: *"The genetic predisposition of **ADHD** is completely overrated."*

Then, as serious as my bully impulsivity managed to curb all the momentum of my verbal irony, I presented to the then columnist, the link of a website, where people, much more reasoned than it, presented arguments (inconsistent, but who already validated more than all this unsubstantiated news) with intent to prove the absence of giraffes. They claim that these animals, when they appear in films, are mere montages, while those of zoos, at best, would be species of robots. And they consider idiots, all those who believe in the existence of the animal. Finally, I explained that perhaps the absurdity that was revealed to her in front of these people who did not believe in giraffes was as incoherent to me as those who do not believe in the veracity of **ADHD.**

However, I must admit that, immensely more ruinous than all this news deleterious, occurs when the discredit arises precisely from those people closest to their reality. As previously reported, in the book *Tendency to Distraction,* Edward Hallowell and John Ratey (1999) mentioned, including, among the first of the most common problems in the treatment of **ADHD:**

> Some people, especially important in life — father, mother, spouse, teacher, boss, friend—do not accept the diagnosis of **ADHD.** They don't "believe" in **ADHD** and don't want to argue about it. It's like it's against your religion or worldview. They make the person with **ADHD** feel a fraud or an impostor. This type of disbelieving response can undermine both the hope that accompanies the diagnosis and the treatment. Variants of the type are often heard: "This **ADHD** does not exist. It's just an excuse for laziness." [...] The important thing is information. Introduce the facts to the person. Stick to the facts, their sit-in to face superstition, rumors, told me, prejudice and misinformation. Try to avoid inflamed debates. It is common to use diagnostic objections to hide emotional issues. There may be anger from the diagnosed person. There may be resentments towards the person for all their mistakes and not if you wish that they escape easily with a diagnosis. They want punishment and so they are increasingly angry at the notion of **ADHD,** trying to make it fall into disrepute. In these moments it is better to stay with science, so stay with the facts we have about the **ADHD.**

At some point feelings of anger should be treated for what they are: anger in general stems from an annoying past behavior on the part of the person with **ADHD.** These feelings are perfectly understandable and valid. However, they should not be used to invalidate a correct diagnosis of **ADHD.**

I also confess — against all my willingness to omit that —the dismay over my condition, has never only been limited to **ADHD.** I have never even had a complicit perception of all the damage that a whole academic life with Dyslexia had cost me. Of the low school income, through the misunderstanding of almost everything I read and/or wrote. Triggering serious problems characterized in the precise or fluent recognition of words, decoding problems, and orthographic difficulties. As Willcut (2001) states, the presence of **ADHD** significantly increases the impairment of reading processing in dyslexic patients: reading requires a considerable level of attention to select relevant information and ignore less important stimuli. People with **ADHD** in comorbidity with Dyslexia have more behavioral problems, lower self-esteem, higher incidence of school dropout, and a worse prognosis when compared to the group with **ADHD** or Dyslexia alone.

Dyslexia is the most common Learning Disorder (A), occurring in about 8% of school-age children. More conservative estimates point to the prevalence of AD in approximately 25% of children with **ADHD.** Both **ADHD** and Dyslexia are associated with multiple neuropsychological deficits, in particular with impairments of executive functions (WILLCUT, 2001).

I do not know if by the absence of self-pity that never incited my vocation to interpret the vitimist — or because for me it has always been given the role of understanding everyone's disorder around me. However, the prevalence of truth is that, without ever realizing the deep embarrassment that that kind of disregard about my condition caused me, on November 25, 2013, I received from a "person very close to my reality", an email with the link of an interview, as absurd and abstract as some mentioned above:

Indiscriminate use of Ritalin can cause 'genocide of the future', says pediatrician.

Indicated to treat patients with attention deficit and hyperactivity **(ADHD),** Ritalin has been indicated uncontrolledly in the country. Currently, Brazil occupies the world's second position of drug use, behind only the United States. In the case of children, who have the organism still in the growth phase, the risk is even greater. "There is a lot of talk that if the child is not treated, it will become a chemical or delinquent dependent. No given allows you to say that. So, you don't have proof that it works. On the contrary: it does not work. And what's happening is that the diagnosis of **ADHD** is being made in a very large percentage of children, indiscriminately," says pediatrician Maria Aparecida Affonso Moysés, a professor at the Department of Pediatrics at unicamp's Faculty of Medical Sciences (FCM). The expert says that if there is no stricter control over the drug, future generations could suffer considerably. "We run the risk of genocide of the future." Ritalin is a Methylphenidate, from the amphetamine family, and aims to improve concentration, decrease tiredness and accumulate more information in less time. It turns out that the drug can bring chemical dependence because it has the same mechanism of action as cocaine and is classified by the Drug Enforcement Administration as a narcotic. Adverse reactions to drug use take place throughout the body and, in the central nervous system, are more incisive. "This is mentioned in any book of Pharmacology. The list of symptoms is huge. If the child has already developed chemical dependence, it may face the abstinence crisis. It may also present outbreaks of insomnia, drowsiness, worsening in attention and cognition, psychotic outbreaks, hallucinations and risk committing even suicide. Data registered in the *Food and Drug Administration* (FDA) are recorded.

Disregarding the nefarious prognosis used as the title of the interview, initially, the slight oversight of the pediatrician in mentioning only the marketing name of one of the drugs, Ritalin, rather than citing them in allusion to its active ingredient, the Methylphenidate hydrochloride, which in addition to covering the trade names of other types of Methylphenidate available in Brazil — would provide readers with a greater understanding of their differentiation in dosages, from the manufacturers' laboratories, and mainly, in relation to its time of action:

a) Ritalin® 10 mg. (Novartis Laboratory): Short-acting methylphenidate, in effect, from 3 to 5 hours;

b) Ritalin ® LA 20, 30, and 40 mg. (Novartis Laboratory): Prolonged-acting methylphenidate, with an effect of approximately 8 hours;

c) Concerta ® 18, 27, 36 or 54 mg. (Janssen-Cilag Laboratory): Prolonged-acting methylphenidate, in effect, from 10 to 12 hours;

By declaring that the drug is "indicated to treat patients with attention deficit and hyperactivity (**ADHD**) — although it may, but should not consider as a serious misunderstanding — the mere omission of the term "disorder" preceding the expression "deficit", already in the use of vowel "and" in the interval of the words "attention" and "hyperactivity", it seems unaware of the existence of cases where the disorder occurs without the presence of hyperactivity. Because of this, even since 1994 the *American Psychiatric Association* (APA) adopted the term Hyperactivity Attention Deficit Disorder, with the use of the bar preceding "Hyperactivity" as a demonstration that the disorder may arise with or without hyperactivity, although hyperactivity is the symptom that defines this picture most. Also, in this same stretch, it also demonstrates not knowing that in addition to **ADHD,** Methylphenidate is used in the treatment of cases of Narcolepsy, and Idiopathic Hypersomnia.

Then, when it states that "Ritalin has been indicated uncontrolledly in the country. Currently, Brazil occupies the world's second position of drug use, behind only the United States." Even not to mention data, prognosis, percentages, statistics, estimates, lies etc. or any kind of resource ahead of their fallacies, as someone with a specialty is expected about what she says, yet she achieves the incredible feat of making serious numerical mistakes by the very dimity of what she does not know. Although between Set. /2011 and Oct./ 2012, methylphenidate consumption in Brazil showed a significant increase of 1,853,930 in the number of boxes sold, there are two antagonistic factors, but equally logical that pediatricians certainly do not know. Or if she knows — unlike the normality of those who know what they're talking about — she preferred to demonstrate her insipidity:

1º. Despite the large increase in the sale of Methylphenidate, if weco-found the data on the prevalence of **ADHD** in Brazil around 17 million people, even with all 1,853,930 boxes, about 30,000 patients would only be being treated with Methylphenidate in the country.

2º. However, it is impossible to know if there really is an excess in the consumption of Methylphenidate in the country, without knowing the amount of the drug being used for the treatment of cases of Narcolepsy and Idiopathic Hypersomnia, the percentage of people diagnosed with **ADHD** being treated with Methylphenidate, guessing (since it is not known) how many boxes are acquired illegally, being able to access the amount of Methylphenidate provided to the Health Unic System (HUS) (which are not accounted for in the studies) to only thus make the correlation between all these data with the prevalence of **ADHD** in the country.

3º. This all disregards that the interviewee completely ignores the aggravating factor of — unlike other countries — there is only Methylphenidate as a drug substance of choice available for the treatment of **ADHD** in Brazil. Which inevitably greatly enhances its consumption.

By vaguely mentioning, as you do during the entire text: "There is a lot of talk that if the child is not treated, it will become a chemical or delinquent dependent. No given allows you to say that. So, you don't have proof that it works. On the contrary: it does not work." Well...As for the excerpt in which the *pseudo specialist* mentions the risks of lack of control, claiming: "[...] if there is no stricter control over the drug, future generations may suffer considerably."

Subsequently, aside from the use of hypothetical expressions, when it states that the drug does not work, in addition to contradicting the numerous scientific articles available, usually in the academic environment when we affirm or disagree with something, we must present some kind of technical and/or scientific resource (research, articles, etc.) to substantiate what we stand for. She, unlike true experts, to support her arguments, does not even use *Wikipedia* as an allegation of its data collection source.

By saying that "Ritalin is a Methylphenidate, of the amphetamine family, and aims to improve concentration, decrease tiredness and accumulate more information in less time. It turns out that the drug can bring chemical dependence because it has the same mechanism of action as cocaine, and is classified by the *Drug Enforcement Administration (DEA)* as a narcotic", the interviewee expresses precisely the opposite of what numerous studies affirm: the efficacy of Methylphenidate has its proven action in reducing symptoms of attention deficit, better performance of motor activities, reducing hyperactivity, controlling impulses, — and to the extreme setback of what it says at random— the use of Methylphenidate, of long-release types, even provide an inhibition of drug abuse.

Already about "reducing tiredness and accumulating more information in less time", or it suffers from some kind of mental alienation, or lacks a reasonable ability to understand some reality outside of her personal opinions. Due to ineptitude, ignorance or incompetence, the pediatrician cites entities with attributions that are not of their competencies. In the United States, the *Drug Enforcement Administration* (DEA) is not the institution responsible for classifying drugs. The DEA's mission is to enforce the laws relating to controlled substances, and to supervise organizations and/or persons involved in the manufacture and/or distribution of these substances. In fact, the *Food and Drug Administration* (FDA), a U.S. health surveillance agency, is responsible for classifying drugs and/or medications.

With regard to the analogy it tries to create between Cocaine, Amphetamine, and Methylphenidate, it is important to highlight that only two amphetamines are legally marketed in Brazil: Dextroamphetamine, and Methamphetamine. And although the three substances have similar Chemical Formulas:

(A)   Methylphenidate ($C_{14}H_{19}NO_2$);

(B)   Amphetamine ($C_9H_{13}N$);

(C)   Cocaine $(C_{17}H_{21}NO_4)$,

They are totally divergent in relation to pharmacokinetics (route of administration, absorption, biotransformation, bioavailability and excretion). They are also distinct as the main chemicals (neurotransmitters) that interact, how they interact. And above all, they act in different regions of the brain. While Methylphenidate acts in the outermost layers of the brain, known as the cortical region (site related to memory functions, attention, consciousness, language, perception and thought), Cocaine and Amphetamine act in the *Accumbens Nucleus,* portion of the "reward system" (one of the main areas responsible for predisposition in chemical and physical dependence). Cocaine and Amphetamine are Monomania Oxidase Inhibitors (IMAO) promote increased availability of norepinephrine and serotonin in the synaptic cleft (space between two neurons). Methylphenidate, in turn, is a Dopamine Reuptake Inhibitor (DRI), however, in addition to not activating the "reward system" acts more in modulating dopamine levels than from Norepinephrine.

Roughly — propagated only by common sense — from which I presume to derive the non-existent knowledge of the pediatrician, it can be said that Methylphenidate works by what is usually called the "paradoxical effect", that is, it is a psychostimulant, but that has a contrary effect.

Even reproduced by journalists and/or non-specialized professionals, not to mention references, report scientific articles, or present any research that validates their lying statements, these types of libelous and alienating subjects - convey to readers a false idea that there may be doubts about the existence of **ADHD.**

Claiming that **ADHD** does not exist, as well as claiming that the drugs used for its treatment are "dangerous" beyond the explicit demonstration of ignorance, can be configured as a crime because it conveys wrong information on public health. Reproducing misleading news, while omitting hundreds of scientific data documenting the benefits, efficacy and safety of medicines used to treat **ADHD**, not only hinders and delays people's access to diagnosis and treatment, but also reveals bad faith, disengagement. to the basic principles of journalism and expresses one of the most perverse forms of discrimination against people suffering from mental disorders and / or disabilities: the Psychophobia.

The World Health Organization (WHO) defines Mental Health as a welfare state in which the individual is able to exercise his skills, manage normal stressful events in life, work productively and contribute to his community. A Mental Disorder, therefore, can be understood as a medical condition that alters this state causing impairment in the individual's overall performance. According to the Brazilian Psychiatric Association (BPA) it is estimated that more than 40 million people in Brazil suffer from some type of mental disorder. Thus, those suffering from Depressive Disorders,

Obsessive-Compulsive Disorder (OCD), Hyperactivity Attention Deficit Disorder **(ADHD)**among so many other mental illnesses begin to feel increasingly excluded, in the face of these types of prejudiced manifestations disseminated by the media.

On the existence and veracity of **ADHD,** it is worth noting that — in addition to being officially recognized by the World Health Organization (WHO) — **ADHD** is also validated by an International Consensus: scientific production published after extensive debates among researchers from different cultures, institution, and that they do not necessarily share the same ideas about all aspects of a disorder. According to the *American Psychiatric Association* (1994) **ADHD** is one of the best studied disorders in medicine, and general data on its validity are much more convincing than most mental disorders, and even many medical conditions.

Currently, **ADHD** is the most frequent reason among children and adolescents referred for care in specialized services. It is estimated that it affects 2.5% of adults, about 3 to 7% of school children (from 6 to 12 years old) worldwide, and in more than 68% of cases the disorder remains throughout life. According to the Diagnostic and Statistical Manual of Mental Disorders in its 5th edition (DSM-V), **ADHD** is more common in males than in females, in the proportion of 2:1 in children, and 1.6:1 in adults. The characteristics related to inattention have a higher incidence in females, while symptoms related to hyperactivity and impulsivity are more observed in males. The disorder also has high rates of comorbidities: in children with **ADHD**, more than 50% of cases arises with the presence of — at least — some other comorbid disorder, and approximately 10% of them, develop three or more comorbidities. Research indicates that among children, the most frequent are:

- Defiant Opposition Disorder — 40 %

- Anxiety Disorders — 34%

- Conduct Disorder - 14%

- Learning Disorders (Reading, Calculus and/or Writing) - 10 to 25%

- Tic Disorder — 11%

- Mood Disorders - 4%

Among adults with **ADHD,** comorbidities affect approximately 70% of patients — of which 97% have up to four comorbid disorders. Studies indicate that for every five adults undergoing treatment for some other disorder, at least one of them has **ADHD.** Among the most common comorbidities observed in adults are:

- Depression — 20 to 30%

- Anxiety disorder -20 to 30%

- Substance use - 25 to 50%

- Smoking - 40%

- Antisocial personality disorder - 25%

- Sleep disorder - 75%

In addition to triggering serious losses of productivity and motivation in academic, vocational activities, as well as a reduced ability to express ideas and emotions, instability in different types of relationships, impairment of execution memory, social retracting, negative effects of the image itself, etc. Hyperactivity Attention Deficit Disorder **(ADHD)** usually causes a series of impacts in the course of a person's life:

1) Adults with **ADHD,** regardless of the level of education, earn salaries significantly lower than adults without the disorder. The study showed that the difference is around $10,000 annually for individuals with higher education and 4,000 for those with only high school;

2) 25% of adults with **ADHD** do not finish 2nd grade against 1% of adults without **ADHD;**

3) Only 15% of adults with **ADHD** attend university against more than 50% of adults without **ADHD;**

4) Adults with **ADHD** less often complete a University;

5) Adults with **ADHD** less often get full-time jobs than adults without disorder. Item accounts for 17% of the $77 billion of projected losses in the study. Generating economic impact on society;

6) About 25% of students with **ADHD** present learning problems in any of these sectors: oral expression, comprehension, interpretation of texts and mathematics;

7) 30% of children and adolescents with **ADHD** repeat at least one school year, multiple repetitions occur in 21%;

8) 35% of adolescents with **ADHD** drop out of school, 45% are expelled from schools and 21% have classes repeatedly;

9) It is estimated that the emotional development of children with **ADHD** is about 30% slower than that of children without the disorder. For example, a 10-year-old with **ADHD** operates at a maturity of 7 years. A young 16-year-old driver with **ADHD** has a profile of decisions of an 11-year-old;

10) 65% of children with **ADHD** present challenge behaviors of authority such as verbal hostility and tantrums;

11) Children with **ADHD** are often victims of head trauma or polytrauma, accidental intoxications and ICU admission as a result of these medical complications;

12) Children with **ADHD** have a 3-fold higher risk of domestic accidents, 2 times higher than trauma, sutures and hospitalizations and 20% of them are responsible for serious fires in their communities;

13) Increased risk of pregnancy before 18 years of age and sexually transmitted diseases in young people with **ADHD;**

14) Young people with **ADHD** have a 4 times higher risk of causing accidents, 7 times higher than multiple accidents and with victims, and 4 times higher the incidence of fines (due to speeding and not respecting traffic signs);

15) Young people with **ADHD** are at higher risk of substance use, abuse and dependence. In a survey, tobacco use was reported by 50% of young people with **ADHD** against 27% of young people without the disorder, alcohol use 40% versus 28% and marijuana 17% versus 5%;

16) Separation or divorce occurs 3 times more among parents of children with **ADHD** than parents of children without the disorder;

17) 49% of children with **ADHD** have difficulties in relating to other children versus 18% of controls (children without **ADHD);**

18) 72% of children with **ADHD** have conflicts with siblings and other family members against 53% of controls;

19) 48% of children with **ADHD** have ease of adaptation to new situations against 84% of controls;

20) 18% of children with **ADHD** reported having good friends against 36% of controls;

21) 52% of children with **ADHD** need parental help in school tasks against 28% of controls;

22) 26% of children with **ADHD** need the help of parents to get ready to go to school against 16% of controls;

23) Comparative studies show that adults with **ADHD** have more often: drug addiction (or drug addiction), suicide attempt, divorce, unemployment, professional dissatisfaction and social misfit.

Celebrities with ADHD

ADHD is one of the most recurrence mental disorders on the planet. From poor to rich, atheist to fanatic and famous to anonymous: there are all profiles of carriers. To break some paradigms about the disorder (such as that it is believed that it prevents someone from being successful and efficient in what they do), see this list with some cases of famous people who own **ADHD**. You may know some cases, but for sure others will be very amazing! Check:

1. **Sylvester Stallone.** Yes. The great, eternal and legendary Rambo has ADHD!

2. **Magic Johnson.** The basket player considered the NBA's top point guard also has ADHD.

3. **Tom Cruise.** Being a (world-renowned) and successful actor with ADHD seems like an impossible mission to you? Not for Tom Cruise.

4. **Jim Carrey.** Jim's case with the disorder is well known around the world. The actor incorporates **ADHD** well with his clumsy and agitated style, don't you think?

5. Prince Charles. The first in line of succession and holder of the Prince of Wales titles in England also know on the skin what it is live with **ADHD**.

6. Einstein. Humanity's greatest genius is a very knowledgeable case of **ADHD**. It clearly shows that the disorder does not prevent anyone from – based on much will, encouragement and effort – achieving efficiency, prestige and recognition.

7. Walt Disney. As difficult as the disorder may be, Walt Disney is the perfect case that being **ADHD** has its advantages, including the free and creative mind (which contributed to the births of the brand classics of the same name as its creator).

8. Pablo Picasso. Picasso was eternized by his unparalleled works, but also leaves a little-known legacy of overcoming **ADHD**.

9. Salvador Dalí. Dali's eccentric manner accompanied the **ADHD** he had. It is further proof that the creativity of the carrier is giant, even forming, of an extensive list of artists who possess the disorder.

10. Caitlyn (Bruce) Jenner. The former transsexual athlete has already been hailed as "the world's greatest athlete" in 1976 during the Summer Olympics in the U.S. and has ADHD.

11. Steve Jobs. Jobs also have **ADHD** and is another case that proves the creative potential of many people with this disorder.

12. Danny Glover. The actor and activist also have the disorder.

13. David Neeleman. The Brazilian businessman, descended from Dutch and American, founder of U.S. airlines JetBlue Airways, Morris Air, Canadian WestJet and Azul Brazilian Airlines also has **ADHD**. Can you believe multi billionaire David has the same inconvenience as other persons with **ADHD**?

14. Adam Levine. Adam Noah Levine is an American musician. He is the lead singer and guitarist of the band Maroon 5. He also participates in the reality show: The Voice - United States. He is a world-renowned case of Attention Deficit Hyperactivity Disorder.

15. Howie Mandel. Howie is an American comedian and creator of the famous "Bobby's World". Coincidentally (or not), the creator of the **ADHD** icon character has the disorder.

16. Jennifer Lawrence. The lead actress of "The Hunger Games" and Oscar winner for best actress also know in her skin what it's like to have ADHD.

17. Justin Timberlake. With a very well consolidated career and unmistakable voice and waddle, Justin proves that a mental disorder like ADHD is not preventing enough for those who know what he wants and makes it happen.

18. Michael Jordan. This **ADHD** carrier is "nothing more, nothing less" than the guy considered the greatest basketball player in history.

19. Michael Phelps. The myth of swimming pools and greatest Olympic medalist in history, Michael Phelps, also has **ADHD**.

20. Michelle Rodriguez. Mayte Michelle Rodriguez is an American actress known for the films The Fast and the Furious, Fast Six, Resident Evil, Resident Evil: Retribution, Avatar, S.W.A.T. and from the famous television series 'Lost'.

21. Sir Richard Branson. Richard Charles Nicholas Branson is a British businessman, the founder of the Virgin group. Its investments range from music to aviation, clothing, biofuels and even aerospace travel.

22. Solange Knowles. Solange Piaget Knowles is an American singer, songwriter, DJ, dancer, actress and model. She's the sister of singer Beyoncé.

23. Will Smith. The disorder did not prevent him from becoming (nothing more, nothing less) than one of the most respected actors in the world, rapper, film producer, music producer and television producer.

24. Bill Gates. Who thought Jobs was alone representing the great world of technology business was wrong: the founder of T.I.'s best-known company, Bill Gates, also has **ADHD**.

25. Tracey Gold. American actress Tracey Gold is also the protagonist of our list of famous people with **ADHD**.

26. Usain Bolt. The fastest man in the world also knows what it's like to be known to be restless... And that led him to a huge number of Olympic medals!

27. Christopher Knight. Christopher is an American actor and closes this list of famous people with **ADHD**.

Testimonials from People with ADHD

I'm Like that

I knew it was different since I was a kid. I was born that way. Is it just me? I'd ask, ask, and there was no answer. I always felt like a stranger in the nest, a being from somewhere other than that. I didn't know, I just didn't know. I've always felt everything to the extreme. Love, hurt, friendship and all the feelings united in one. Sadness and joy smile and crying, curiosity and indifference. By the way, curiosity is what moves me. It's a curiosity from the simplest and most beautiful to the most unknown. It is a thirst for constant knowledge, even if it is not for an obvious goal. It is knowing, to understand, to answer the many "whys" of life.

I have doubts about everything. Past, present and future. Research, research and research and never settle for what people say just to shut me up. It's something like inexplicably loving the unknown. It is to be at the height of a right choice and abandon everything in search of the new. It's feeling alone in the middle of a crowd and feeling inserted in a context, being part of the world, even though I'm isolated in the room. It's fighting with my brother and stopping everything because I remembered that I bought him a medallion, in a church, on the same day. Deliver, explain how you use it and then fight again, but stop all over again because I didn't remember the reason for all that.

Is loving life!!! Wanting to live intensely every moment, and loathe the way people live, because deep down, deep down, I feel very different from everyone else. It's buying a gift for someone for no reason just because I'm happy, but not knowing why so much happiness. And when I try to remember why, I fall into deep sadness because I realize that everything is temporary.

I hate rules and norms, but I try to comply with them because I have respect for others. I talk to people I've never seen in my life, but sometimes I'll put a friend away talking to himself just because I remembered something through a word he said. And I run away because I had a lot of miraculous ideas about it, really magnificent. With several thoughts at such a great and crazy speed that when I stop to write and organize everything, it's over. I've forgotten because in fact the sequences of thoughts are so intense that I lose myself in time. I lose the notion of time and space.

I can't rest in my sleep, so I get tired all day after, but when the night comes again for me to sleep, I get a total pike. It's so much energy, I don't know where it comes from and then I invent a lot of things to do and distract myself. I wake up wanting something, throughout the day I want another 50 and, at bedtime, I put everything aside because I already have a passion for a new idea. And I do everything I can to make it work, but then I see it didn't work out because I've given up.

I cry for the problems of the world, without at least solving mine. And I laugh in the middle of a serious meeting and soon I regret it because of the consequences. It's like I'm a child despite the responsibilities and missions to do.

I focus on a new subject as if it were the salvation of the world and I end up putting aside the chores that would save me the day. , without destiny and right direction. It's all very broad, the thoughts are broad.

In fact, no one around can understand me, and I don't even know how to explain. I can't do it. I lose friends for not being understood, but I understand all of them because I actually feel different and do not know how to explain why. But now I know why. It's all very confusing and I love being like this because if God made me with this little in my brain it's because I have a very different mission to accomplish and I just still don't know which one.

By Flávia Mendes Gomes

Books on the Bookshelf

My room is a rat nest. All of a sudden, I get out of bed on a jump and put everything in its place. So, it's my heart, too. I try to get the books on shelves: one, for family people: daughter, husband, parents, brothers. Another, friends: those who are gone, those who are always close, those who have never been, but who love as much as others. Another, the acquaintances: people who come and go once or again, but who have made no marks. Another, the enemies: which ones? I have many of them. But I never know who they are. For me, everyone is good, they only make mistakes sometimes.

Then, after three days everyone is together on the same shelf, the labels got lost, I don't know who's who, who's from where. Wait a minute! That sounds like my office. (laughs).

My life is like this: everything has its place, but they change constantly. And then I don't know where they were from anymore, so people mix. Friends become family. Enemies, they become friends, and so you go.

It's confusing, but it's kind of good. With memories, that's the way it is, too. I hear one story, I remember another one, read one word No day is the same, because when he is born just like yesterday, I'm already different. Humor? I've got a lot. Bad mood, too... (laughs). I'm captivating with my talking way. But I'm tiring when I talk beyond the bill.

My stories are always the most fun, illustrated with gestures, sounds, mimes, etc. at least, I strive to the fullest. When I read a book, I enter the story: if it's raining in the tale, when I close the book, I run to close the windows, as if it were raining there, too. On the other hand, if the book is bad, I skip pages and go straight to the end.

Movies then... They're a problem: I hate watching alone, but nobody wants to watch with me. After all, my nickname turned out to be "cricritic", because each scene deserves a comment. Everything I do has to be the best. Being good, just, it's not enough for me. And if what you're doing isn't enough to be the best, wide in half and I don't finish anymore.

I love recognition and praise, but I love doing them, too. When I'm criticized or reprimanded, I always give an explanation. My fights are always fleeting. After all, I end up forgetting why I fought. I look at people and I know what they're thinking. Especially what you mean to me. I have lapses of imagination. I look at one thing, and I imagine a direct relationship with something else, which usually has nothing to do with everything has to have to do what and why!

I worry about what others think of me, so I do everything in the best possible way. I do five things at the same time now, when I get carried away in one of them, I dump all the others without remorse. I never forget God, I avoid asking, but I always do a morning. I'm extremely emotional. I'm crying just watching someone sing well at Raul Gil, can you? When I talk about people I like, they never have flaws, just qualities.

I wake up in the middle of the night to remember that I forgot my Uncle Kiko's birthday that was three days ago. Oh! But I remembered three dawn before the day, too. I love being philosophical, paradoxical. I observe graffiti drawn on the city walls and try to imagine what was going on in the head of those who designed it. What did he try to say? Am I crazy? Or, just disorganized ideas, really?

I guess I haven't forgotten anything, from I? So, the conclusion is for you to take it off.

Thatiana Nunes, 26 years old, publicist, married and mother of Giovana, with just 2 little years. Resident of São Paulo — capital, clinically diagnosed with ADHD, and never made use of Ritalin. At least to date, November 17, 2005.

ADHD Outburst — A Cry of Self-Knowledge

You know that child everyone thought was kind of "crazy", who did everything at the same time, with fleas in short, springs on his feet and a self-rechargeable stack?! Yes, it was me! I even think the character "Little Boy" had to be me, "Gisele — The Little Girl".

As a child, I only hung out with the boys because I always thought girls' games were boring and dull. And because of that I was always tasked with things like " *imp*" and " Male woman", but I never cared much for these things because I, even as a child, knew that it was not that and took in the joke or made me a plea.

I've always hated rules and I'm not much of a good thing about complying with them, especially those I don't agree with, or I don't understand why I follow them. During class I was always talking or up to some —tacks, gum, paper balls, tying laces of others and other gutters to colleagues or teachers. But I only took good grades and despite all this, the worst teachers (who all students hated because they were demanding) liked me. The director doesn't even talk... I lived on the board of punishment, and Loved it, because -- at least -- I'd have lunch and talk all afternoon with the main.

Curious to the extreme, I always wanted to know why things, how they worked and I have personal taste for different and unusual things. I could spend hours doing something, almost on another planet — usually doing things that other people thought was difficult — and for other things It distracted me from the noise of any pin falling to the ground. I've seen myself in a lot of trouble or embarrassing situations for it.

I almost always had the solution to some problem that no one could solve and wanted to put into practice, which always put me as a leader of group and room, even though I was "rebellious". But sometimes I get in the way of simple things, which my former boss says, "Swallow the elephant, but you choke on the mosquito...". My head is like a whirlwind of ideas... I only had one little problem: I kept forgetting things like important dates, commitments. I prefer a thousand proofs to a written job, because I always forget to do them.

For a "sleeper" child this scenario is even common, the point is that there is no way to describe a person's entire life in a brief text and the details of these and other situations only people who have **ADHD** can know. With all this childhood record, I got some stigmas: "She's not going to be anything in life if it goes on like this...", "Black family sheep. This one I don't know, saw..." and even my sexuality doubted that they liked the things boys liked because they were more active.

Although I'm already an adult, I still have many of these characteristics with "Rayovac", which I have been with since childhood. I took my life to date constantly dealing with "labels" and funny nicknames. I'm used to it and I know how to deal well with them being a humorous person and getting into the game. I've always felt a little or a lot: crazy, smart, forgotten, different, insane and fun. Almost everyone I know think I'm am fun, and they consider me a good friend for who I am and accept me like this, even though I can't understand myself most of the time. I understand that, since I can't even understand myself sometimes.

I found out about the **ADHD** by chance. I saw that a "virtual friend" had and, because I was curious, I researched what it was about. I read a subject from a medical site: " Attention Deficit Hyperactivity Disorder **(ADHD),"**Extracted from the book: ***Transform your brain, transform your life — by Daniel G. Amen.*** And as I read, I practically saw my life being described in every line of that text. Although long, I read in a few minutes (hyperfocus) and when I finished my hands were shaky and my head at a thousand an hour. I needed to make sure if I had **ADHD** or not before jumping to conclusions.

I researched more about the subject, Marcus Deminco was a great friend in this process, because he clarified to me several, doubts and appointed me a very ethical professional — Dr. Paulo, whom I also owe a lot, who, after consultation, diagnosed me as a **ADHD** of the functional type, since I can work, study and live with the situations of life, and so I do not need to take *Ritalin* and / or other remedies.

It is difficult for a person to spend his whole life being different, especially considering how humanity treats who or what is different, and at the age of 23 discovering a part of what makes him so different is shocking, but at the same time liberating. I think that's the feeling I had and I imagine I could have lived up to my last days on earth without ever knowing that I had **ADHD** and that others may be in worse conflicts than mine — since I was very lucky to know how to deal with the bad things of the **ADHD** and enjoy the good things.

I told my family, that it didn't show much surprise, since I was never very normal. And many of my friends don't believe or don't take seriously what I say about the **ADHD** and I have, when Marcus told me that He was writing this book on **ADHD** I was very happy, because being a book by someone who has **ADHD**, could pass an equal -- or at least similar -- that of other people who also go to these through same situations.

I continue to research about and exchange my experiences with others who have **ADHD.** With our fun, difficult and unusual situations, but above all: with the certainty that our life will never be simple, because we have come to give and see a special color to everything, because in fact, the life of a person who has **ADHD** is far from normal, common and common. And with these exchanges of experiences we can understand each other better and others to live better as well.

Gisele Reis, 24, Information Technology Administrator (IT). In addition to designer, coordinator of technological projects, dancer, counselor, commercial assistant and other things more... Like almost every good ADHD that has various affinities and abilities.

The ADHD Self

He always asked me if all others also lived with "thoughts a thousand"; if they kept thinking at any time; associations were made at all times with anything; if they had mood swings and emotions all the time; if they always lived "in the world of the moon". I began to understand my questions at the age of 18, when I knew how to be **ADHD** and I saw that the way i acted and lived was all "normal" for an **ADHD** being.

It is wonderful the cascade of emotions that you feel; the drastic and rapid change of mood; the countless amount of thoughts and ideas that passes through the speed of light through the mind; the inexplicable creativity that "appears out of nowhere" and takes over its being; love him passionately and madly.

It's horrible the fear of not working; insecurity; be aware that you forgot something, but not know what; feel like an worthless, a useless, a excluded one that does not fit into society with its strict rules; suspect that your friends don't consider you so much you consider him.

Love so intensely that at all times one wishes to tell the loved one how he feels for him; always buy something that reminds you of the loved one, sometime lived, some comment heard, or merely some "crazy" association that only you understand yourself; think to have found the ideal person and perfect for you, the one to stay together until the end.

Love so simply and banally that you forget about that dinner scheduled for days; who greets the loved one in such a cold way that it generates the impression of no longer loving; that not of attention in the moments that the companion needs to speak.

The impulsivity of wanting to do something for yesterday; without taking a break to measure the real importance of the fact. But how many times and how many times in the middle of that "urgency" remembers something else very important, much more urgent than what is being made, but along the long road that leads to the place where the last to do will take place, the tireless mind diverts us to another door in order to accomplish something else.

Lie down in bed and often try to look for a "Stand By" button, a button to turn off your mind, to stop thinking and let sleep take over. The agony, because in the rush of everyday life when you get a little time at lunchtime to relax, the mind does not accompany the body, does not stop. And when you're getting to sleep, the alarm clock rings.

For me "mental journeys" are the characteristics that most alter my way of being and acting. Like, for example, when seeing a red pen remember a person, the perfume he wore, of complete conversations we had in his house, on the comfortable couch of his living room. And from the sofa arise a souvenir of the ride with the shopping shops, looking for new furniture home. And from the mall remember that movie you watched after you went wrong in a test. And from then on, until the moment comes when you realize the long time that was lost in the daydreams. It can also be dangerous as often in traffic focuses on a particular object and for a few moments lose attention in cars.

Being **ADHD** is living in the extreme. Either a man or a mouse. Do not stop using the mind to the point of generating the exhaustion of this, in which the only thing that is needed is rest. I can't imagine my life any other way. It is true that in many ways we have to keep controlling ourselves, so we don't make any mistakes. I'm happy being **ADHD** and I don't think it would be funny if I stopped being.

By Filipe Ramo Barra

My name is Flavia, and my 9-year-old son Felipe has ADHD

At two years or even less, Felipe made mischief who looked funny and at the same time strange for his age. He was cheerful, had and has to this day an "enlightened" smile. When I was four, he went to school, and in less than two months, I had to take him out because he was always hurt and no one would explain to me why. I put him in another school. It was two years thinking that it was bad, unable to deal with more "active" children, until I took it again. We then went to third school, where he stayed for another two years. At this point, I felt embarrassed to go to school twice, at least, a week, to talk to teachers and principals about his behavior. Aerial, aggressive, messy, what was expected of me, because that was not my son. My Philip was and is a happy boy, good with life, radiant, and irresistibly charming.

I avoided jumping out of the car at the school entrance sign because I'd have to hear whispers and see glances directed at my son aggressively from the children's parents. Another school that didn't know how to handle the problem. The funny thing about this school is that he took more than fifteen warnings and thought it was fun, he came home happy, crazy to show, because even in the face of everything he went through, humor and joy always were constant.

In the next school, I spent all my son's problems, opened my heart with the psychologist of the institution, who proved super-receptive (until then, nor does he imagine that he would be have

ADHD), that no child discriminate was against. At first, I felt good, but over time, I saw my son falling apart, sometimes falling into tears, self-esteem down there. I started looking at more and found out the school doing horrors. Instead of helping him, they took him out of the room (he was eight years old still in second grade) and took him to kindergarten class, where his four-year-old cousin studied and said that if he behaved like a baby, that's where he was going to stay. It was such the humiliation, that I had my son without the mood for nothing for a few days, just sadness. The main and school owner said no one liked him. Anyway, there were so many things, I saw him faltering, suffering, no friends. That hot joy, so soft, was disappearing... Needless to say, once again, in the middle of the year, I took him out of school and obviously I'm moving proceedings against it.

Finally, after this journey, I found a school where, once again, still afraid, I opened my heart. Then Yes, I found a school that welcomed him, when I first heard that my son could be a **ADHD.** I sought help, studied the subject and to this day

Diagnosed, today he has a quiet life. I do not see the **ADHD** as a problem, I see it as a light, a gift, something that being discovered at the beginning, being treated well and accompanied, provides a lot of peace to the **ADHD** and the family. Understanding made me calm down and find out the size of the treasure I have. It's hard still in a few moments but seeing it quiet is something that gives me strength and helps me take the calm and patience i need to understand and adapt to this life so "messy."

I believe that the **ADHD** leads a quieter life, being:

Surrounded by love, do not pamper;

Surrounded by care, without exaggeration;

Being heard, always;

Being understood daily;

Being helpful, useful, without being put aside thinking that with your fob ado way, things will fall, break, mess... The **ADHD** is a normal person like everyone else, but with a LIGHT that makes it special, just a smile to see!!!

____

By Flávia Maria Saldanha

I learned more from my kids than I taught.

At 27 I had my first daughter. The pink, quiet, sweet, doll named Camila. Motherhood was ravishing, a whirlwind of deep love, inexplicably greater than anything that the human being can one daydream of feeling something so wonderful that he soon wanted another child.

Gabriel arrived only 9 years after much waiting and asking God to get pregnant again. I can't put into words the outburst of happiness that took over me, my husband and my daughter, who always asked me for a brother. But life preached me some pieces... Camila has always been so quiet, organized, methodical, introspective, shy and cool, that I suspected there was something wrong there. A mother feels it. And I wasn't mistaken. Soon came the diagnosis of Asperger Syndrome (for the laity, the softer type among autism spectrum disorders — ASD).

But nothing in this world prepared me for everyday life and left me as bewildered as creating a hurricane named Gabriel. Before, we were a quiet, quiet, serene family. Soon things would be completely different and opposite... I realized I was in trouble when one afternoon, I put Gabriel to sleep. We were just me and him at home. My daughter at school and my husband at work. He was only nine and a half months old. I sat in the living room and watched TV.

Suddenly, looking at the ground, there he was, crawling, half crawling at my feet. I screamed scare! My first thought was that there was someone else at home who pulled him out of the crib. I ran into his room and was shocked by what I saw. He had placed close to the grill of the crib, the mischievous, on top of the straw, on top a teddy bear and on top a cradle protector. He made a ladder, went upstairs and then threw himself. He fell to the ground (I didn't hear anything) and he didn't cry. And he went to the living room to meet me. It was the first time I had the feeling that bigger surprises awaited me. And again, I was right.

He walked at 11 months. I moved everything, broke everything, went up, jumped, ran, screamed, burst, got up off the ground and kept running. He broke bones, teeth, tore nails, was always patched with stitches. I lived in the emergency room. He always had bruises so much he ran and got hurt. I stayed behind, attentive, trying to protect him, but he was more agile, faster, more disobedient and wouldn't listen to me. Came the idea of putting him in a school (in the nursery), because he was 2 years old and I believed that there he would burn his energy and have little friends.

Time or time again I appeared by surprise and saw his class sit, lined up, listening to the instructions, the school's stories... But... Where's Gabriel who was never there like the others? I soon spotted him running through the courtyard, with the desperate monitor behind him, flying from one place to another. It wasn't long before he was "invited" to retire. They weren't ready for such energy. I decided to put him in swimming. The teacher apologized and confessed not to realize... So, let's go to football. He paid attention to the ants, butterflies, the clouds of the sky, less on the ball and no one wanted him on his team, because he had no idea what he was doing there, since during the coach's explanations, he was scattered, running across the pitch. For everyone's relief, I decided to get him out of there. Let's try *taekwondo*. Discipline, rules, a rigorous and determined teacher... He asked for clemency two months later.

Gabriel was over classing, sticking the lines, couldn't wait and talk all the time. Good... We still have the sneakers. The balls flew in everyone's heads nearby. The racket also acquired wings and flew away. Again, he stuck lines, laughed too much, talked too much, ran too much and played less tennis... How about English? The school was the most commented in Sao Paulo, prepared only for children. The price of salting any pocket, but I wanted to try everything to occupy it, insert it socially.

Gabriel has always been fascinated by video game, mobile phone, computer. One day an English schoolgirl decided to take an electronic game and unhappiness did not allow my son to touch his toy. Frustration is not something he knew how to handle well... In five minutes, I was back in school, seeing by far the deep hate fults of the boy's parents, who had his glasses broken in his own nose, with a kick that according to Gabriel, he learned in a drawing... Again, he was "invited" to withdraw... He was already 8.

I'd jump from doctor to doctor. Therapy in therapy. Everyone said the same thing: **ADHD** with aggravating in impulsivity and Oppositional Defiant Disorder (ODD). I was driving my car with a shoe being thrown in the head by Gabriel. I'd swallow my lunch so I wouldn't take my eyes off him for a minute. I'd do anything running and distressed to come back close to him and watch him, afraid he'd get hurt. I was going to the bathroom with the open door. He took minute baths. He slept with one eye open and another closed. He supervised the pointy and cutting things of the house. I wash the windows with bars. I'd take the rugs off the floor so he wouldn't trip. I held his hand very hard when we were walking down the street. He always wanted to let go and run away. Going to the supermarket with Gabriel was asking me to stress out. He opened his arms and passed the shelves knocking down everything that came in front. What I put in the cart he'd take and throw away. Going to the movies was a waste of time. He didn't sit and talk loudly all the time.

In the restaurants, he ran and several times, he dropped the trays of the waiters with headbutts. I'd pick up fried chips and shoot the people who were sitting around us. Hanging out with him was a pain in the. I tried to punish you, talk, ignore, be very angry, promise rewards if his behavior was appropriate, but nothing... Nothing was fulfilled, he wouldn't even listen to me. The only thing that made him more focused was the Methylphenidate he took and that was a blessing in our lives.

He once told me that with the medication he could hear what people had to say, because he wouldn't stop a second to pay attention to anything... He spent seven years in high school, and it was seven difficult years. The coordination, the teachers, the board, the employees were excellent. They had touch, preparation, patience and a lot of skill with my son, but it wasn't like that with the schoolgirls and their families. I was always pointed out. Mr. Judged. Doomed, doomed. It was my fault that I didn't know how to raise that boy. At the time of the school break, it was reached to the point where my son had a security to accompany and watch him, since he was very ready in that short period of time. If I told the tears I shed, the nights I went through, the moments of despair, frustration, the fights with God, with the world, the people I eliminated from my user vivacity because they couldn't stand or understand Gabriel, the infinity would be too small to measure.

Nothing had prepared me for such a hyperactive son, so full of energy, so electric. I decided to put him in judo. Again, time and lost money. No one could take it. Although I often lost patience (I'm human), I defended my son with nails and teeth because I knew what **ADHD** was and had the real perception that he had no fault for being and acting like that. It's a neurobiological disorder. It's stronger than him, but much smaller than my tireless, unlimited, immeasurable and unconditional love for him.

The desire to help him turned me into someone else. I went to study, research, devour books. I participated in a thousand congresses, lectures, seminars, meetings, forums that discussed **ADHD**. He was still medicated, with a psychiatrist, with therapy, but he was still an atypical child. He came in causing it in the places;

In high school all I could get away from the classroom was too restless to sit for hours...

At the age of 13, tired of trying so hard to have friends (because it was the way it was, I ended up scaring these "friends"), one day I caught him crying. He hugged me and told me he threw the towel. That no one understood him and couldn't stand to try to make friends anymore. That no one liked him. God knows what I felt at the time. I cried along with him, talking calmly and explaining to him how he was loved by all of us. I've always tried to raise your self-esteem, but there was no way. He was himself and never wanted to be friends with anyone again. For him only virtual friends, this he has many in online games, where he is a beast and quickly learned to read and write in English (better than in English).

One day I decided I needed to do more for him, and I looked for a regular school that had a special room and it was the best thing I did. Gabriel himself told me that he had finally realized that he was not the different "only" that there were others like him. Relaxed, never suffered *Bullying* again. He continues to hate his studies, saying that the school is nothing more than a prison, but is more adapted, with classmates who understand it and are similar to it. Today it is much better, less electric, more centered, more controlled. It's childish for your current 17 years. He has a real obsession with the computer (hyper focus) and his knowledge there is immense.

He's a beautiful boy, loved to the extreme for me, his father, his sister. I could never explain this rapturous love, which cheers me the days, which by seeing it makes my heart accelerate, which immediately brings a smile to my face. He and Camila are the reason for my life. A love for all eternity. I thank God for the privilege of having had two special children who taught me to grow up as a human being and to be a better person. I opened a Parent Association called *'Inspiree'*, with other mothers who also went through all this. Here in São Paulo I try to cherish parents with guidance and support that I did not find anywhere when my children were little. I, for some reason I don't know, have been chosen doubly and i am honored by this opportunity.

I also thank Marcus Deminco for the chance to leave my testimony here and be able to tell novice and young parents that there is a light at the end of the tunnel. That you need to chase knowledge, information and have a lot, but a lot of patience, because the rest only love solves.

Simone Alli Chair, 52 years old — São Paulo/SP. CEO of the Association of Parents Inspiree, President of the Kangaroo Institute (rare diseases), graduated in Social Work, popular defender, militant in the area of disability, but above all and all, Camila's mother, 25 years old Asperger Syndrome, graduated from the faculty of animation design and Gabriel, 17 years old, attending the year last of high school, with prospects of trying to design college in games, her passion. It has ADHD, with aggravation in impulsivity, Oppositional Defiant Disorder (ODD), and recently also diagnosed within the Autistic Spectrum. In treatment with a neurologist and a psychiatrist.

From destroyed self-esteem to Unstable Relationships: ADHD Can Destroy A Life.

I know very well what I've been through, and I'm still going to go today. I was born in 1971 and without understanding about **ADHD** and professionals who at that time did not exist (and there are few to this day) I had my whole life impaired. Without understanding why, even though I'm so smart on issues like creating and fixing things, because just in observing the functioning of things I'm able to disassemble and make it work again because they are situations that we have time to think, analyze the functioning and solve the problem without pressure, which usually does not happen in schools. And so, I grew up, with people always praising me for being creative, intelligent, etc.

But when I went to school, the thing was very different, I only stood out in the matters of fine arts and drawing and always as the best in the room, but in almost all other subjects I was terrible, but it was terrible not for being able to learn but for taking a while to understand and memorize how the other colleagues who took the subject faster, I was sad and always asking myself, "Am I stupid?"

In the classroom when the teacher asked, "Who didn't understand?" I kept quiet, because seeing that all the other schoolgirls had learned I was embarrassed and afraid to be called a donkey, but my low grades, and the need to paste colleagues denounced me and that's how I ended up being seen.

I'm sure if I'd had a different teaching, with people who knew about **ADHD,** things would be different and I would not have gone through everything I went through, because in my learning time respected and with a differentiated teaching methodology, I would have much more success in life, because I would have learned everything, even with all my lack of attention and difficulty in memorizing, because in my time I always learn everything, otherwise the consequence of this was to be phobia by classrooms and job even in job tests that make me sweat cold to this day.

On top of that, many are fears that reach a carrier of **ADHD**. Above all, with regard to relationships and future children... At least that's how it was with me, even though I struggled to forget, hoping that one day things would change, but unfortunately that's not how it happened. Sooner or later you end up realizing that all your fears are fulfilling gradually and the way you always feared.

I imagined having children and at school they would ask you about the subjects you never had the opportunity to learn as you should, due to your **ADHD**, your wife in disbelief about the disorder, not accepting and still saying that there is nothing wrong with you and if that wasn't enough, even buying a car became a distressing problem, when it should be a source of happiness, but it turns out not to be, because even being a good driver the difficulties in memorizing roads and understanding quickly certain street intersections me. It makes you fear going to far places, traveling with the car so don't even think! And so, I just use the vehicle to go to familiar routes.

My ex-wife charged me at the points where I couldn't go any further, and so I also created an almost phobia behind the wheel, simply for fear of new places and finally, the less you want the thing to get worse, come abandonment, she tells you that it doesn't give anymore , and the most frustrating thing about all this is knowing that it wouldn't have been like this if I didn't have the **ADHD**.

So the great need for early diagnosis, as I would now look for a partner with the same disorder, or when starting a relationship with a person without the disorder, would explain about **ADHD**, show stories that talk about it and hope that The partner understands and accepts my limitations, because with the help and not demands and criticism, can make any **ADHD** carrier overcome all the difficulties they may have in life.

Daniel Rêgo de Aguiar (Salvador/BA), 44 Years Old, Security and graduated in ADM Assistant— Diagnosed with ADHD and In Treatment.

Final Considerations

The World Health Organization (WHO) defines Mental Health as a welfare state in which the individual is able to exercise his skills, manage normal stressful events in life, work productively and contribute to his community. A Mental Disorder, therefore, can be understood as a medical condition that alters this state causing impairment in the individual's overall performance. According to the Brazilian Psychiatric Association (BPA) it is estimated that more than 40 million people in Brazil suffer from some type of mental disorder. Thus, those suffering from Depressive Disorders, Obsessive-Compulsive Disorder (OCD), Hyperactivity Attention Deficit Disorder **(ADHD)**among so many other mental illnesses begin to feel increasingly excluded, in the face of these types of prejudiced manifestations disseminated by the media.

On the existence and veracity of **ADHD,** it is worth noting that — in addition to being officially recognized by the World Health Organization (WHO) — **ADHD** is also validated by an International Consensus: scientific production published after extensive debates among researchers from different cultures, institution, and that they do not necessarily share the same ideas about all aspects of a disorder. According to the American *Psychiatric Association* (1994) **ADHD** is one of the best studied disorders in medicine, and general data on its validity are much more convincing than most mental disorders, and even many medical conditions.

Currently, **ADHD** is the most frequent reason among children and adolescents referred for care in specialized services. It is estimated that it affects 2.5% of adults, about 3 to 7% of school children (from 6 to 12 years old) worldwide, and in more than 68% of cases the disorder remains throughout life. According to the Diagnostic and Statistical Manual of Mental Disorders in its 5th edition **(DSM**-V), **ADHD** is more common in males than in females, in the proportion of 2:1 in children, and 1.6:1 in adults. The characteristics related to inattention have a higher incidence in females, while symptoms related to hyperactivity and impulsivity are more observed in males. The disorder also has high rates of comorbidities: in children with **ADHD**, more than 50% of cases arises with the presence of — at least — some other comorbid disorder, and approximately 10% of them, develop three or more comorbidities. Research indicates that among children, the most frequent are:

- Defiant Opposition Disorder — 40 %
- Anxiety Disorders — 34%
- Conduct Disorder - 14%

- Learning Disorders (Reading, Calculus and/or Writing) - 10 to 25%

- Tic Disorder — 11%

- Mood Disorders - 4%

Among adults with **ADHD,** comorbidities affect approximately 70% of patients — of which 97% have up to four comorbid disorders. Studies indicate that for every five adults undergoing treatment for some other disorder, at least one of them has ADHD. Among the most common comorbidities observed in adults are:

- Depression — 20 to 30%

- Anxiety disorder -20 to 30%

- Substance use - 25 to 50%

- Smoking - 40%

- Antisocial personality disorder - 25%

- Sleep disorder - 75%

In addition to triggering serious losses of productivity and motivation in academic, vocational activities, as well as a reduced ability to express ideas and emotions, instability in different types of relationships, impairment of execution memory, social retracting, negative effects of the image itself, etc. Hyperactivity Attention Deficit Disorder **(ADHD)**usually causes a series of impacts in the course of a person's life:

24) Adults with **ADHD,** regardless of the level of education, earn salaries significantly lower than adults without the disorder. The study showed that the difference is around $10,000 annually for individuals with higher education and 4,000 for those with only high school;

25) 25% of adults with **ADHD** do not finish 2nd grade against 1% of adults without ADHD;

26) Only 15% of adults with **ADHD** attend university against more than 50% of adults without ADHD;

27) Adults with **ADHD** less often complete a University;

28) Adults with **ADHD** less often get full-time jobs than adults without disorder. Item accounts for 17% of the $77 billion of projected losses in the study. Generating economic impact on society;

29) About 25% of students with **ADHD** present learning problems in any of these sectors: oral expression, comprehension, interpretation of texts and mathematics;

30) 30% of children and adolescents with **ADHD** repeat at least one school year, multiple repetitions occur in 21%;

31) 35% of adolescents with **ADHD** drop out of school, 45% are expelled from schools and 21% have classes repeatedly;

32) It is estimated that the emotional development of children with **ADHD** is about 30% slower than that of children without the

disorder. For example, a 10-year-old with **ADHD** operates at a maturity of 7 years. A young 16-year-old driver with **ADHD** has a profile of decisions of an 11-year-old;

33) 65% of children with **ADHD** present challenge behaviors of authority such as verbal hostility and tantrums;

34) Children with **ADHD** are most often victims of head trauma or polytrauma, accidental intoxications and ICU admission due to these medical complications;

35) Children with **ADHD** have a 3-fold higher risk of domestic accidents, 2 times higher than trauma, sutures and hospitalizations and 20% of them are responsible for serious fires in their communities;

36) Increased risk of pregnancy before 18 years of age and sexually transmitted diseases in young people with **ADHD;**

37) Young people with **ADHD** have a 4 times higher risk of causing accidents, 7 times higher than multiple accidents and with victims, and 4 times higher the incidence of fines (due to speeding and not respecting traffic signs);

38) Young people with **ADHD** are at higher risk of substance use, abuse and dependence. In a survey, tobacco use was reported by 50% of young people with **ADHD** against 27% of young people without the disorder, alcohol use 40% versus 28% and marijuana 17% versus 5%;

39) Separation or divorce occurs 3 times more among parents of children with **ADHD** than parents of children without the disorder;

40) 49% of children with **ADHD** have difficulties in relating to other children versus 18% of controls (children without **ADHD**);

41) 72% of children with **ADHD** have conflicts with siblings and other family members against 53% of controls;

42) 48% of children with **ADHD** have ease of adaptation to new situations against 84% of controls;

43) 18% of children with **ADHD** reported having good friends against 36% of controls;

44) 52% of children with **ADHD** need parental help in school tasks against 28% of controls;

45) 26% of children with **ADHD** need the help of parents to get ready to go to school against 16% of controls;

46) Comparative studies show that adults with **ADHD** have more often: drug addiction (or drug addiction), suicide attempt, divorce, unemployment, professional dissatisfaction and social misfit.

About The Writer

Marcus Deminco (Salvador-BA. Set, 28 1976). Brazilian writer and psychologist; Doctor Honoris Causa in Attention Deficit Disorder/ Hyperactivity Disorder; Practitioner and Tutor of Neuro-linguistic programming (NLP); Portal of Psychologists Newsletter Subscriber. Wrote several texts, phrases and thoughts shared on numerous websites and social networks. Author of 'Why read Paulo Coelho?' Praised and shared by Paulo Coelho himself among his readers. Marcus Deminco is author of:

1) Me and My Friend ADD - Autobiography of a guy with Attention Deficit Disorder.
2) The Secret of Clarice Lispector
3) VERTYGO - The Suicide of Lukas (Portuguese Edition)
4) VERTYGO - The Suicide of Lukas (English Edition)
5) Neuro-Linguistic Programming: beginning by the beginning.
6) Messages to Post, Like and Share. Vol. 1
7) Messages to Post, Like and Share. Vol. 2
8) Messages to Post, Like and Share. Vol. 3
9) E-cards text collection. Vol. 1
10) E-cards text collection. Vol. 2

Awards and Tributes

1.1. Author of 'Estafeta Sem Rumo' – Cecilio Barros Barros Pessoa Awards of Anthology – Academy of Letters, Arts and Sciences of Arraial do Cabo - RJ.

1.2 Doctor Honoris Causa in ADHD by the Brazilian Association of Psychosomatic Medicine in recognition of the scientific contribution and social relevance of the book: Me & My Friend ADHD – Autobiography of a guy with Attention Deficit Disorder.

1.3. One of the winners of *Além da Terra, Além do Céu* prize of contemporary Brazilian poetry awarded by Chiado Editora.

Talk to Marcus Deminco

E-mail: marcusdeminco@gmail.com
Website: http://marcusdeminco.com/
Blog: http://marcusdeminco.blogspot.com.br/
Twitter: https://twitter.com/marcusdeminco
Facebook: https://www.facebook.com/marcus.deminco
Pinterest: https://www.pinterest.com/marcusdeminco/
Instagram: @marcusdeminco
Youtube: https://www.youtube.com/channel/UCRu8yfSoLewjuX6GO6o7Nmw
Tumblr: http://deminco.tumblr.com/
Flickr: https://www.flickr.com/photos/143729713@N06/with/28004881736/
GoodReads: https://www.goodreads.com/author/show/7792932.Marcus_Deminco/
Pensador: https://pensador.uol.com.br/autor/marcus_deminco/

www.ingramcontent.com/pod-product-compliance
Lightning Source LLC
Chambersburg PA
CBHW061245140726
47998CB00006B/2106